Original title:
Tales from the Thistles

Copyright © 2025 Creative Arts Management OÜ
All rights reserved.

Author: Dexter Sullivan
ISBN HARDBACK: 978-1-80567-245-6
ISBN PAPERBACK: 978-1-80567-544-0

Touchstones of the Teasel

In a garden of thorns, a fool found his way,
Strumming laughter like strings on a bay.
A thistle with tales, sharp spines made him yelp,
He danced with the weeds, and he tripped on himself.

The creatures all chuckled, each leaf gave a grin,
As he stumbled and fumbled, let the antics begin.
A butterfly snickered at his flailing feet,
"You're quite the performer, a real treat to meet!"

With a twirl and a swirl, he flipped through the grass,
Tipped over a pot and fell on his... sass.
The daisies all giggled, their petals in flight,
For the fool in the thistles was quite the delight.

So gather the blooms, let the laughter unfold,
In the realm of the sharp, the stories are bold.
With prickles and chuckles, we all just agree,
Life's far more amusing when you're silly as me!

Portraits of the Untamed Green

In a garden wide and bright,
Sassy weeds dance in delight.
They giggle and sway with glee,
While flowers roll eyes at the spree.

A dandelion dons a crown,
Looks quite regal, never frown.
As bees buzz by, they take a chance,
To join in this ridiculous dance.

Grass gets jealous of the crew,
Pokes fun at each bold debut.
But under the sun's golden sheen,
All laugh together, it's a scene.

With thorns that prickle, thistles tease,
A wild party, quite the breeze.
Each leaf seems to join in the laugh,
Nature's comic relief, a great photograph.

Ryzen of the Resilient Root

In the soil, the roots reside,
Underneath, they love to hide.
Whispering jokes of pasts they've known,
While birds above just moan and groan.

A beetle claims he's got the moves,
Says he's groovier than the grooves.
Then trips over a fallen leaf,
Wriggles away, part of the beef.

The carrots boast their orange pride,
"Don't you wish you were this side?"
But radishes snicker from below,
"We're under the earth, still in the show!"

While whispers swirl through air and root,
A laughter-rich, loamy pursuit.
Each moment grows, a wicked gleam,
In this underground comic scene.

Epics of the Garden's Edge

At the edge where daisies stand,
Ants march out, their little band.
With tiny swords, they lead the way,
In their world, it's all fair play.

Ladybugs with polka dots,
Challenge crickets in funny knots.
Who can hop or fly the farthest,
In a battle that's rather heartless?

The produce rooters cheer and shout,
As beet veggies spin, there's no doubt.
Lettuce hats that flit and fly,
With every spin, they curve and sigh.

But the weeds roll their eyes, ask why,
This whole digging dance? Oh my!
As the sun sets, the laughter fades,
In the garden where fun parades.

The Thicket's Silent Vigil

In shadows deep, the bushes plot,
An opera show, but they forgot.
The stage was set, yet none showed up,
Except for a lone raucous pup.

With twigs and sticks as makeshift fans,
The thorns drew seats, not high demands.
But laughter echoed in the air,
A silent vigil, full of flair.

Burrows beneath, the rabbits peek,
At thistle threads that tease and speak.
"Are we in for a monster show?
Or just a giggle? Let's not toe!"

The thicket's kind, a secret place,
Holding tales of a leafy race.
Where humor thrums like a violin,
In wild entwinements, joy begins.

Tales of the Tansy

In a garden once lively and bright,
Tansy danced with delight.
She wore a crown made of bees,
Tickling legs and swaying leaves.

The gnome laughed at her bold style,
Said, "You wear pollen with a smile!"
She swirled like a merry sprite,
Making flowers sigh with delight.

One day she tripped over a thorn,
Crying, "Oh, why was I born?"
The daisies chuckled, 'You're so spry!'
Just get up and give it another try!

At night she'd glow, a star on the plot,
Challenging crickets to dance, why not?
With twinkling eyes, she'd call to the moon,
"Come join our frolic, we'll dance till noon!"

Chronicles of the Cow Parsnip

Cow Parsnip sat with a grin,
Holding court with a wild spin.
"What's next on our list today?"
"A game of hide and seek, hooray!"

Beneath the stars, they all conspired,
To hide where the frogs had retired.
"Don't peek, or you'll spoil the charm!"
Laughed the fox, without any harm.

As shadows leaped from blade to blade,
Cow Parsnip squeaked, 'I'm so afraid!'
But giggles burst from friends around,
Every rustle a joyous sound.

At dawn, they'd rise, their fun complete,
With tales of mischief, oh so sweet.
"More games tomorrow, what do you say?"
Cow Parsnip grinned, brightening the day!

The Mythos of the Mint

In a patch where the mint leaves thrive,
 Minty whispers come alive.
 The ants like to form a parade,
 Singing songs that never fade.

One day Mint thought to take a chance,
 And invited the bees to a dance.
 They buzzed and twirled all around,
 Creating a sweet, sticky sound.

But then came a gust, a wild breeze,
 Sweeping the ants and the bees.
Mint fumbled and tumbled down the hill,
While everyone laughed and cheered with will.

At sunset, they settled and sighed,
 "I'm minty fresh!" Mint proudly cried.
 With laughter echoing near and far,
 They promised adventures 'neath the stars.

Whispers from the Wisteria

Wisteria sighed in violet hues,
Dropping petals like morning dew.
"Listen closely, I have a tale,
Of a very odd snail named Gale."

Gale wore glasses too big to see,
Said, "Why rush? Life's meant to be free!"
He wandered off, lost in a dream,
While others plotted and schemed.

The ladybugs laughed, what a sight!
"No urgency, just pure delight."
With a wink and a nod, they drew near,
"Join us, dear snail, there's fun here!"

The moon rose high, their laughter soared,
Snails and flowers together adored.
Wisteria whispered, "Oh what a night!"
"Who knew slow could be such a delight!"

Dances with the Dandelions

In the breeze, they swayed and spun,
Little yellow faces, oh what fun!
With every tickle, a giggle flies,
As dandelion fluff begins to rise.

They join a waltz beneath the sun,
Whispering secrets, just for fun.
Each twist and twirl, a puff released,
A dance with weeds, a wild feast!

A parade of petals, a joyous sight,
In gardens where all things feel just right.
The bees are buzzin' in happy trails,
While curious ants share gossip tales.

So here's to the blooms with the laughter bright,
In the kingdom of green, they steal the light.
With dandelion dreams floating in the air,
Life's just a party, come and share!

Echoes of the Echinacea

In fields of pink, a sneaky joke,
Echinacea laughs, as the flowers poke.
With petals that giggle and wiggle about,
They whisper sweet nothings, casting doubt.

In the summer sun, they throw a ball,
Come one, come all, the fun's for all!
A game of hide and seek, quite absurd,
Where bees are referees, buzzing unheard.

They sway to a tune, a delightful scheme,
Planting mischief like a daydream.
Each blossom a jester, grinning wide,
Making the garden their jolly ride.

So if you wander in their merry dance,
Take a moment, give laughter a chance.
For in this patch of playful scenes,
Echinacea echoes our wildest means!

The Chronicles of the Clover

In the shady greens, the clovers play,
Spinning stories through the day.
Each leaf a tale, they weave with cheer,
Whispers of luck for all drawing near.

With a wink and a nod, they glow and shine,
Prancing around in a vibrant line.
Four-leaf wonders with secrets to tell,
Spin yarns of giants, they do it so well.

Their laughter echoes in the warm sunlight,
As Ladybugs join in, taking flight.
With mischief in tow, they dance in a row,
Creating legends we all wish to sow.

So stop for a moment, take a good glance,
At the clovers who invite you to dance.
For in their chronicles of joy and delight,
Every heart can find its light!

Legends of the Lush

In the realm where the green leaves play,
Legends unfold in a funny way.
The ferns gossip in a gentle breeze,
Trading jokes with the buzzing bees.

Over by the brook, a frog steals the show,
With leaps and bounds, moving to and fro.
While brambles chuckle, tickling the air,
And every critter joins in with flair.

The blossoms join in, with colors bright,
As nature's stage becomes a sight.
Each rustle and giggle, a tale they weave,
Inviting all who dare to believe.

So stroll through the lush, let laughter flow,
Discover the magic that only they know.
For within every leaf and each playful swirl,
Lie legends of joy in this green, wondrous world!

The Tale of the Thrift

In the garden, thrift we find,
Always a bargain, never blind.
It wears a crown of dandelion,
With roots that play, a wild medallion.

The squirrels share a funny cheer,
As it dodges a hungry deer.
Growing tall on a patchy spot,
It whispers secrets, quite a lot.

When winds blow strong, it shakes a jig,
Turns the soil into quite a big gig.
The dance of greenery's delight,
Makes the evening a comical sight.

So here's to thrift, a funny friend,
In the garden, joy won't end.
It thrives on laughter, sprightly glee,
Among the thorns, so wild and free.

Murmurs in the Meadowlark

The meadowlark sings in bliss,
Chasing shadows with a twist.
Its chirps are tales from sky to earth,
Creating giggles, giving mirth.

A butterfly joins the frolic dance,
Stumbling over its own romance.
With each step, a funny glide,
Nature joins in, a joyous ride.

The daisies nod, they can't resist,
As bees buzz by, they can't assist.
They tumble down, a sight so sweet,
In the fray of laughter, they find their beat.

And when the evening paints the sky,
The meadowlark lets out a sigh.
With every note, a chuckle shared,
In the meadow, joy is declared.

Revelations of the Rockrose

Rockrose stands in proud array,
With petals like a bright ballet.
It tells tales of silliness abound,
In every breeze, a giggle found.

A bumblebee, so round and fat,
Tries to woo a fluffy hat.
It buzzes low, it sways a bit,
While rockrose laughs, it won't permit.

When raindrops fall, they skip and hop,
On rockrose tops, they never stop.
Each splash a joke, each drop a pun,
Beneath the clouds, the day is fun.

So here's to laughter in the bloom,
Rockrose spreads cheer, like sweet perfume.
In every whisper, a story told,
Of joyful moments, brave and bold.

The Harmony of the Helianthus

Helianthus, the sunflower bold,
Greets the day with stories untold.
It nods to friends on every side,
In a sunny dance, a joyful ride.

With petals bright, it shows a grin,
Waves to the bees, lets laughter in.
A wink to clouds, a giggle so loud,
It's never shy, always proud.

When evening comes, it bows down low,
But not before a final show.
It spins and twirls in twilight's glow,
Creating joy in the afterflow.

So raise a cheer for sunshine fun,
Helianthus shines, the day is won.
With every turn and every sway,
It brings the smiles, come what may.

Whimsy Amidst the Wildflowers

In the meadow where daisies dance,
A butterfly sneezed, oh what a chance!
It startled a squirrel perched up high,
Who tumbled down with a comical cry.

The bees wore hats made of soft petals,
While ants in suits played tiny kettles.
A rabbit juggled carrots with glee,
As the sun giggled, shining down free.

The flowers formed a band with pride,
Each note a burst of colorful stride.
The tulips twirled, the roses spun,
As laughter echoed, everyone had fun!

So join the dance beneath the sky,
And let your worries flutter and fly.
In this garden where joy beads,
Each bloom whispers the best misdeeds.

The Legend of the Larkspur

Once in a garden, quite far away,
Lived a larkspur with things to say.
It wore a crown made of twinkling dew,
And told funny tales of a frog that flew.

It claimed that sparrows stole its shoes,
And danced with crickets to chase away blues.
Each night it crooned songs to the moon,
While the fireflies joined, a syncopated tune.

But one day it slipped on its own petal,
And tumbled down like a wild, raucous metal.
The weeds all chuckled, "What a sight!"
As the larkspur grinned with pure delight.

In the lore of flowers, its fame still grows,
A clumsy prince in a kingdom of prose.
With laughter and blooms, it's here to stay,
Spreading joy in its own quirky way.

Melodies of the Marigold

In a patch of gold where marigolds sing,
The daisies joined in, it's quite the fling!
They formed a choir with voices so bright,
   Making even the ants tap with delight.

A ladybug spun in a floral swirl,
While butterflies twirled, giving wings a whirl.
The sunflowers laughed, their heads held high,
   As the petals confetti'd down from the sky.

"Oh hear the tune of the thirsty bee,
Who buzzes and hums a sweet harmony!"
The garden blooms as a stage so wide,
With each flower ready for a comedic ride.

So come and join this playful crowd,
Where each little bloom is cheerful and loud.
In this vibrant garden, fun never grows old,
   For it dances to life in hues of gold.

Epics of the Evening Primrose

In twilight's glow, the primrose glows bright,
Whispering stories beneath the starlight.
It giggles with shadows, casting its spell,
Of critters who pranced, oh what a swell!

A cricket recited poetry grand,
With a snail as his muse, so steady and planned.
The moon chuckled softly, a patron of night,
As the flowers swayed, a comical sight.

The firefly glimmers like stars in a jar,
While the hedgehog declared he'd drive a car!
He rolled and he tumbled, oh what a mess,
In a wild adventure, they couldn't care less.

Under the primrose, dreams start to play,
With giggles and chuckles, they romp and sway.
So dance with the night in this whimsical maze,
Where every shadow sparkles and plays.

Whispers in the Weeds

In a patch where daisies grin,
The hedgehog wears a silly fin.
The rabbits dance in moonlit glee,
While ants prepare a grand jamboree.

A squirrel's tale gets told with flair,
Of how he found a missing chair.
With acorns piled all five feet high,
He claimed the throne and waved goodbye!

The thistles laugh, their spines so proud,
As butterflies go floating loud.
A beetle juggles leaves galore,
While ladybugs just roll on the floor.

Oh, the mischief in the shade,
Where friendships form and pranks are made.
In whispers soft and giggles shared,
The weeds unite, no trouble bared.

Through the Twisted Briar

Beneath the brambles, oh what fun,
A hedgehog rides a wheel of bun.
A ferret plays his favorite tune,
While rabbits hop beneath the moon.

A grumpy fox with fur all fluffed,
Sells lemonade, his stand is stuffed.
He shouts, "Come try my sour blend!"
While every sip causes a trend!

The brambles tangle tongues of cheer,
As every critter draws so near.
They giggle loud, they squeak with flair,
Until the evening breezes fair.

With dance and laughter, oh so bright,
The briars twirl in sheer delight.
A celebration timed just right,
In shadows deep, beneath the light.

Echoes of the Thorned Path

In the thicket where echoes play,
A hedgehog hums a funky sway.
With thorny friends in close embrace,
They form a band, a wild space.

A badger dons a feathered hat,
While chasing down a playful cat.
The thorns they poke with gentle tease,
As laughter floats upon the breeze.

A startled jay begins to squawk,
While rabbits gather 'round to talk.
With tangled tales and jokes that sting,
The path resounds with what they bring.

So join the hall of thorny jest,
Where every twist is surely blessed.
In echoes bright, the vibes align,
With all the fun, the stars will shine.

Secrets Beneath the Stinging Bloom

Beneath the blooms that seem to glare,
Are secrets kept with subtle care.
A snail shares tales of long-lost shoes,
While bees recite their buzzing blues.

In shadows deep where critters scheme,
A fox concocts a wild, strange dream.
He winks and nods, "It's not what's seen,"
With a glance at blooms, so fresh and green.

The flowers nod in whispered jest,
As bumblebees just can't quite rest.
So tipsy on the nectar sweet,
They twirl around in endless beat.

Secrets linger in the air,
While creatures frolic everywhere.
With laughter bold, the blooms will share,
Their stinging joy that's beyond compare.

Reflections in the Prickly Abyss

In a garden full of spines, so bright,
A hedgehog wore a hat, what a sight!
He danced with glee in the afternoon sun,
While bees buzzed along, just for fun.

The thorns held secrets, sharp tales untold,
Of flowers that whispered, of petals so bold.
A snail in a shell claimed he was a knight,
But he fled from a squirrel, oh what a fright!

Rabbits debated who was the best,
In tail-wagging contests, they put it to the test.
The thistles just chuckled, so clever and sly,
Hoping to catch one, oh my, oh my!

With laughter and pranks woven into the air,
The garden became a circus, beyond compare.
So if you wander where laughter grows thick,
Beware of the thistles, they'll pull a good trick!

Riddles in the Bramble's Embrace

In a bramble so tangled, a riddle was spun,
A fox in a scarf thought it all was such fun.
He puzzled the rabbits with riddles and rhymes,
While fluttering butterflies danced out of time.

A bumblebee buzzed, with a question quite sly,
"Why do the daisies look up to the sky?"
The daisies just chuckled, their petals so bright,
"Because the sun's dapper, he makes them feel right!"

The hedgehogs assembled, a council so grand,
To crack the great mystery of this wild land.
With thorns as their pens, they inked in the lore,
And laughed at the riddles, always wanting more.

So next time you wander through thickets so lush,
Listen close, you'll find giggles that make your heart rush.

For in every thorn lies a joke or a jest,
Just waiting to tickle the mind and the best!

Memories Among the Sharp Florals

In a patch of sharp florals, where memories bloom,
A cat with a crown thought she ruled the room.
She pranced like a queen, with a tail held high,
While the cacti just teased, as spiky as pie.

A robin recounted her wild escapades,
Of chasing her dreams through sunlit glades.
The daisies rolled over in fits of pure glee,
As shadows danced lightly and teased through the tree.

A bumble bee traded old stories and tales,
Of grasshoppers jumping and epic pail sails.
The thistles all chuckled, "Oh please, just one more,"
While the daisies piled on, in this vibrant uproar.

So lift up your heart and embrace the bright scene,
In gardens of laughter, where humor reigns keen.
Among sharp florals lies joy uncontained,
In memories cherished, forever unfeigned!

Journeys of the Ensnared Petals

Oh, the journeys of petals, so soft and so bright,
Yet caught in the thistles, what a hilarious sight!
One petal proclaimed, "I'm a ship on the lake!"
While tangled in brambles, a grand frolic to make.

A butterfly laughed, with her wings all aglow,
"Take care, little petal, from thistles, don't go!"
But adventure called out, with a giggle so sweet,
As petals waltzed onward, oh where would they meet?

The thorns seemed to snicker, with secrets to share,
Of blossoms that wandered but stuck in mid-air.
Who knew that a journey could wrap you so tight,
While spinning through laughter beneath the moonlight?

So cheer for the petals, their mischief and cheer,
In the land of the thistles, where giggles appear!
They may be ensnared, but their spirits won't fall,
For in every adventure, they stand proud and tall!

Ballads of the Bounty

In the garden where veggies sprout,
The carrots debated what they were about.
Tomatoes blushed with their juicy pride,
While radishes claimed they'd never hide.

One pumpkin advanced with a frown,
Said, "I'm the king, you all just clown!"
But the beans just laughed, swinging their vines,
Said, "Your royal crown is full of twines!"

The squash did a jig, it danced on the ground,
While peas shouted, "Hey, we're lost, not found!"
A cabbage rolled in, with a leafy cheer,
Saying, "Let's all join for a veggie beer!"

So they laughed and they played till the day was done,
In this quirky patch, they knew how to run.
With chummy debates and laughter galore,
This garden of joy was never a bore.

Chronicles of the Chrysanthemum

In a pot on the shelf sat a flower so bright,
Who dreamed of the sun but craved the moonlight.
The daisies would gossip, whisper and tease,
While the hungry tulips begged for some cheese.

One night they all giggled, snickering in glee,
As the spider spun tales, quite sloppily.
"You think you're the best? Oh, what a mistake!"
Said a rose, with thorns, "I'm the queen of this lake!"

Yet a sunflower yelled, with a grin ear to ear,
"You all look so silly, it's perfectly clear!"
They roared with laughter, what a funny show,
In flower land, shades of color would glow.

As the moonlight danced, under starry beams,
They told weird stories, fueled by their dreams.
With petals a-bouncing and roots filled with cheer,
The chronicles spun with laughter sincere.

The Lore of the Lavender

In a field where the lavender whispered so sweet,
The bees wore tuxedos, they danced on their feet.
They buzzed near the blooms, with tales to impart,
While the flowers all crowed, "We're the bestest art!"

A butterfly swooped in, landed quite bold,
"I'll paint you all dreams in colors of gold!"
But a sleepy old bug snored, dreaming of pies,
"Hey, keep it down! I want to dream 'til I rise!"

The lavender chuckled, then swayed in the breeze,
"You can nap, dear friend, just don't sleep on the peas!"
While the daisies snickered, sharing their jokes,
With rhymes and with riddles, they teased the good folks.

When the sun dipped low, and laughter rang clear,
They wove a bouquet of jokes that brought cheer.
With scents of fun swirling, a whimsical race,
In the lore of their laughter, they found their place.

Verses of the Violets

In a patch of bright violets, problems arose,
One claimed to be famous, from bookshops and prose.
The others just laughed, "Oh, you think you're a star?
We've got roots in the ground; you just dance from afar!"

A snail with a shell, slick and so snail-like,
Proposed they all share stories, just like a bike.
"No need for a rush! We'll take it all slow!"
The violets retorted, "You'll make it a show!"

Now the violets plotted, with giggles and grins,
They feasted on pollen and shared silly sins.
"You're a flower, I'm a slug, what a curious pair!"
Said a violet sprightly, with a flair and a glare.

As night cloaked the garden, a party began,
With laughter and whispers, oh, what a plan!
These verses of joy, where odd friendships bloom,
Made the world brighter, dispelling all gloom.

The Spirit of the St. John's Wort

In the garden, it dances bright,
With petals that giggle, a silly sight.
Whispers of laughter, the bumblebees share,
As they buzz around without a single care.

When sunlight kisses each little leaf,
The grasshoppers join, their tune beyond belief.
They hop to a rhythm, a vibrant charade,
While St. John's Wort beams in the fun parade.

A curious fox peeks from behind a bush,
Chasing butterflies in a cheerful rush.
The flowers all chuckle, they can't help but jest,
In a world where silliness is truly the best.

So if ever you find yourself feeling blue,
Just dance in the meadow, join the laughter too.
For in this garden, jokes grow like weeds,
And the Spirit of Wort plants the funniest seeds.

Secrets of the Sedge

In the marsh where the wise sedge grows,
It tickles the toes of ducks on their toes.
They quack out the secrets, oh what a tease,
As the wind weaves in whispers, so silly it flees.

The frogs hold a meeting, dressed quite absurd,
In ties made of reeds, how utterly blurred.
They croak their conclusions, a chorus of cheer,
Claiming the marsh as their comedy sphere.

With each playful splash, the sedge starts to sway,
As if it's chuckling at the frogs' silly play.
A turtle rolls over, giggling with glee,
In the theater of nature, what a sight to see!

So come to the marsh, take a seat on the bank,
Where laughter flows freely, and joys never tank.
For the secrets of sedge are a song of delight,
Where fun never fades, and the day ends just right.

Ghosts of the Goatsbeard

In the twilight glow, where the Goatsbeard sway,
The silhouettes dance in a most comical way.
With shadows that frolic, they whisper and tease,
As the breeze carries giggles from trees to the bees.

"Who's there?" asks a cow with a puzzled frown,
To the specters who twirl in a fluffy white gown.
"Just us," laugh the ghosts, with mischievous flair,
"Telling tall stories if you care to share!"

They rattle their hooves, make the stars jiggle bright,
As the moon beams above, bathing all in soft light.
With echoes of laughter, they spin and they twirl,
Painting the night with a ghostly swirl.

So if you find yourself near the meadow at dusk,
Listen for chuckles, find adventure and husk.
For the Goatsbeard is whispering secrets so grand,
Where ghostly fun reigns, and joy holds your hand.

The Saga of the Snowdrop

Out pops a Snowdrop, brave and so white,
From blankets of snow, what a curious sight!
Shivering slightly, it giggles with glee,
"I'm the first little flower! Come see me, come see!"

With bravado it nods to each gust of wind,
Making friends with the heat that winter has thinned.
The robins do chuckle, as they hop to and fro,
At the antics of Snowdrop, putting on quite a show.

It calls to the snowflakes, "Why don't you stay?"
As they melt into puddles, in laughter they sway.
The sun beams down, with a wink and a grin,
As Winter steps back, and the fun can begin.

So each spring when you see that bold little bloom,
Remember its courage, dispelling the gloom.
For in the saga of Snowdrop, you'll find,
Life's funniest stories are often unrefined.

The Journey of the Juniper

A Juniper danced on a breeze,
With one leaf tickling a bee's knees.
It laughed as it twirled in delight,
While the bee buzzed away in a fright.

The squirrel cheered from a branch high,
"Oh Juniper, how you catch the sky!"
But slipped on a nut, rolled down fast,
And landed in moss that was soft as a cast.

They laughed at the mess they both made,
As the sun set and shadows played.
Juniper shrugged, what a ruckus,
With a giggle, "Let's blame it on the focus!"

As night fell, 'neath the starry show,
The Juniper whispered, "Time to go!"
The bee, now dizzy, flew in a loop,
They all agreed—what a silly group!

Rhapsody in the Rousers

In gardens bright, the Rousers sang,
With pants so loud, they often rang.
They danced like ribbons caught in the breeze,
Making each flower giggle with ease.

A ladybug stopped, tapped on a toe,
"Please, oh please, don't steal the show!"
But the Rousers twirled, swished with flair,
While butterflies watched and joined in the air.

"Oh what a crowd!" the dandy dahlia cried,
"Come join our fun, don't hide!"
With petals bursting in laughter and glee,
The Rousers spun wild—now that's a spree!

At last, they collapsed in a heap on the grass,
With giggles and puffs, what a silly class.
So here's to the Rousers, so bold and spry,
In a world where laughter will always fly!

Anecdotes of the Anemone

The Anemone waved in the tide,
With stories of fish that took pride.
"Oh, once I saw a crab do a jig,
With flippers that flapped and danced like a pig!"

The seaweed chuckled, "What a strange sight!"
As dolphins leaped far into the night.
"Tell us again!" all the sea critters cried,
With excitement that grew like the rising tide.

As starfish clapped with all of their might,
Anemone spun in the shimmering light.
"Then there was Bob, the forgetful old eel,
Who thought he was slick, but slipped on a wheel!"

They roared with laughter, salt in the air,
"Next time, Bob, move with a little more care!"
The tales went on beneath the bright moon,
With each splash and giggle, we sang a new tune!

The Odyssey of the Orchid

An Orchid set out on a quest,
To find out which flower was best.
"I'll win with perfume and petals so fine,
Just watch as I dazzle, I'll surely shine!"

The Daisy scoffed with a wink and a smile,
"Competing with me? Please, stay awhile!"
But Orchid swirled with a cheeky glow,
"I'll show you all how it's done, you'll see, just so!"

Through gardens she pranced, adorning her grace,
While Tulip grinned, just loving the race.
Each twist and each turn brought humor and cheer,
As they tripped over humor, not one shed a tear.

At sunset, they gathered, exhausted but bright,
"I guess we are all truly a delight!"
The Orchid laughed, "Let's stop this charade,
What matters most is the fun that we've made!"

Myths from the Thicket's Edge

In the thicket, shadows play,
Where the critters have their say.
A squirrel wears a tiny hat,
While rabbits chat about their cat.

A hedgehog tells a daring tale,
Of how he rode a gusty gale.
The porcupine pranced in glee,
Claiming to be a bumblebee.

The owl hoots, wise and loud,
But can't remember where he plowed.
A fox sneezes, breaks the spell,
As everyone starts to yell.

They laugh till the moon is high,
With stardust flinging through the sky.
In the thicket, humor reigns,
As whimsy dances in their veins.

The Dance of the Whispering Vines

In the garden, vines entwine,
They giggle as they twist and twine.
A grape jokes about the wine,
While sunflowers sway, feeling fine.

The tomatoes boast of being red,
While lettuce dreams of a fancy bed.
A cucumber slips, what a scene,
Saying, "I just wanted to be green!"

The daisies twirl in joyful glee,
While roses sing in harmony.
With whispers of a breeze so sweet,
The garden's got them on their feet!

They dance as shadows start to play,
Hoping fun might come to stay.
In this patch, none are shy,
Each petal's laughter fills the sky.

Memoirs of the Jagged Leaves

Jagged leaves on the forest floor,
Whisper secrets, tales of yore.
A maple leaf claims it can fly,
While oak chuckles, "Give it a try!"

The wind gives them a playful shove,
They tumble and twirl, full of love.
A pinecone laughs, "I'm the best!
Just look at me, I'm one of the rest!"

With every crinkle, stories spin,
Of autumn's grace and winter's grin.
A witty seed says, "Watch my leap!"
As the forest bursts with laughter deep.

In the chorus of nature's tune,
They joke with the warm afternoon.
These memoirs of humor weave,
In every rustle, they believe.

Songs from the Barbed Fringes

From the barbed fringes, tunes arise,
With brambles sharing quirky lies.
A thorny bush sings like a pro,
Teasing weeds that dance below.

Stickers share a prickly joke,
As thistles giggle and poke.
A dandelion dreams to soar,
While nettles plan a prank galore.

The sun sets on this ragged crew,
As shadows start to stretch anew.
With laughter echoing through the night,
These songs fill the air with delight!

Each prick and poke, a funny tale,
In the wild where humor won't fail.
With spiky rhythm and sharp refrain,
The fringes sing of joy and pain.

Stories Held in Thorny Embrace

In the garden of giggles, thorns stand tall,
With prickly jokes that make you fall.
A dandelion's wink, a rose with sass,
Oh, what a show! You can't let it pass.

Cacti wear hats, made of bright sunbeams,
Their party's a riot, bursting with dreams.
Sunflowers dance with daisies in tow,
While violets suggest, 'Let's steal the show!'

Bumblebees buzz in their striped attire,
Making everyone laugh as they conspire.
"To pollen, or not? That's the real question!"
And they answer with joy, their sweet concession.

Each thorn has a tale, each petal a pun,
In this wild plot twist, who's winning? Just fun!
Nature's a jester, in colors so bright,
Laughing through gardens, from morning to night.

The Chronicles of Nature's Resilience

In the heart of the forest, where mischief grows,
Moss tells stories that everyone knows.
With crickets as scribes and owls that narrate,
Each chapter a giggle, a twist to celebrate.

Raccoons steal snacks, beneath the wild moon,
While squirrels hold meetings, plotting by noon.
"Who'll climb the highest? Who'll get the best nut?"
Their laughter resounds, in a cheerful rut.

The winds share secrets, whispering light,
A butterfly giggles, takes off in flight.
"Do I look good in this dress of bright hues?"
Each one's a comedian, spreading the news.

And under the stars, with a wink and a nod,
The flora and fauna play on, unflawed.
The chronicles twinkle, through ages they sway,
Nature's resilience? A humorous play.

Whispers of the Weeds

Behind the fence, where wild ones creep,
Weeds share their whispers, secrets they keep.
"Did you hear what that nettle just said?
It's a riot, I swear, it's better than bread!"

They gather in circles, a mischievous bunch,
Laughing at daisies, "They're all just a punch!"
A thistle declares, with a smug little grin,
"Who needs a garden when chaos can win?"

The grass rolls its eyes, "I'm so over this life,
Where are the hearts? Where's the true strife?"
But the clovers just giggle, "You're too uptight,
Join the fun, dear friend, we'll dance through the night!"

So amidst the patch, where wild laughter flares,
Whispers of weeds float on soft, fragrant air.
"No prunes and no rules, just frolic and play,
In this patch of mischief, let's brighten the day!

Secrets in the Shadows

In dim-lit corners, where shadows conspire,
Fungi giggle softly, igniting their fire.
"Did you hear what the moss said to the root?
'You're looking a bit wobbly, grab some fruit!'"

Under the ferns, a plush fairy sneezes,
While spiderlings weave webs that bring pleases.
"Catch a breeze, dear friend, come dance in delight,
Nature's a party, by day and by night!"

A rogue toad croaks, with a voice so divine,
"Why don't we hop, and create a new line?
To the beat of the rain, we'll twirl and we'll spin,
With laughter and joy, let the frogging begin!"

Each shadow a story, each rustle a smile,
In this secret realm, make memories worthwhile.
So listen well, for the whispers are clear,
Nature's sweet secrets beckon us near.

The Secret Life of Burgeoning Briars

In a garden not too far, a thistle had a dream,
To dance beneath the stars, a rather funny scheme.
It wiggled with delight, and off it went to soar,
But owls thought it was lunch—oh, what a dreadful chore!

So the thistle donned a mask, a leafy disguise,
Pretended to be waxed, to hide from hungry eyes.
But giggles filled the night, as critters passed it by,
'What's that leafy creature? Just a shrub that's trying to fly!'

Each thistle told a tale, of pranks it surely played,
Of snipping at the roses, and how they felt betrayed.
'These stems are just like us,' the daisies rolled their eyes,
'Creating little dramas under sunny, silly skies.'

A thistle's life is wild, a thorny rollercoaster,
With prickles on the side—oh, what a funny roaster!
So next time when you see them, don't just pass them by,
Wave to those prickly pals, they'd love a friendly hi!

An Anthology of the Prickly Path

On a prickly path they marched, a troupe so full of glee,
With dandelion hats and thistle ties, what a sight to see!
They sang of sweet mischief, of blunders big and small,
'The rose thinks she's so grand, but just wait till she falls!'

Cacti joined the dance, with a shimmy oh so bold,
But each step they took was quite painfully controlled.
The daisies rolled their eyes, saying, 'What's that rude display?'
'Prickly folk just like their thorns, let's keep them far away!'

With every laugh and snicker, more blooms began to join,

A petunia flipped her curls, with a wink and a coin.
They twirled and spun around, through thicket, bush, and bramble,
But their antics kept them stuck, a thistle's awkward scramble!

So if you hear a ruckus, don't be shy or mute,
Just peek behind the fence, at this prickly, fun commute.
There's humor in their struggle, these plants know how to play,
Life's not just about the blooms, it's all about the sway!

The Melodies of Stubborn Stems

In the garden's lovely hum, the stubborn stems proclaim,
Their rhymes of gentle teasing, and a very silly game.
'Come listen to our song,' said the thistle with a grin,
'We've tales of all the weeds, and how to pull them in!'

A stubborn stem sang loud, 'I will not bend or sway!'
While thrumming in the breeze, it just wouldn't go away.
With petals sharp and proud, it proclaimed, 'I am the king!'
Yet a gust of wind said, 'No! Your crown is but a fling!'

The daisy giggled soft, 'Oh, listen to the strife,
These stubborn stems are funny, it's a comical life!'
As vines began to twist and twirl, under the moon's soft light,
They laughed at all the mischief, till day broke in the night.

So here's to those wild stretches, those stems that refuse to bow,
To the flowers that keep singing; let us all take a bow!
For in gardens full of laughter, the blooms will surely sway,
Together in their antics, they brighten up our day!

Vibrations of the Untamed Flora

In a tangle of wild vines, the flora had a chat,
'What's life without some giggles? Come join my fluffy spat!'
They bumped and pushed each other, with no care for the fuss,
'The daisies are just jealous, they can't match our robust!'

With each bump and vibrant twist, they jiggled in delight,

Creating silly dances, under the pale moonlight.
Spinning tales of crazy weeds, and fables from the past,
The story of a thistle who got caught in brambles fast!

Buds burst into laughter, petals fluttered bright,
'We're not just untamed flora, we sparkle in our right!'
With every twist of humor, their fragrance filled the air,
'Just don't step on our toes, or we'll give you quite a scare!'

So if you wander near, and hear their raucous cheer,
Just know it's joyful laughter, not a reason for a fear.
The plants may look so prickly, but inside their hearts beat warm,
In the dance of wild relief, they find comfort in the swarm!

Chronicles under the Chicory

A mouse wore a hat made of chicory leaves,
He danced with the ants and played tricks with the thieves.

The beetles all laughed, their shells shiny and new,
As the lizard sang songs that no one ever knew.

Under the clouds of a cotton candy sky,
A snail told a tale, to a fly buzzing by.
With a puff and a spin, they twirled in delight,
While the grasshoppers grooved in the warm summer night.

A squirrel with a scarf tried to juggle some nuts,
Fell in a pile, oh, the silliness cuts!
The daisies would giggle, their stems all a-shake,
As the sun sneered back, peeking over the lake.

Every creature a star in their whimsical play,
In the kingdom of thistles, they danced all day.
With laughter and cheer, they'd put on their show,
In a world where the funny things always would grow.

Reveries of the Redbud

A raccoon named Ron wore a bright purple tie,
He'd tell all his friends he was classy and spry.
With a wink and a grin, he'd steal from a dish,
Claiming it's art, as he swirled in a swish.

The cardinals chirped in a crazy old chorus,
Of baked beans and laughter, how could you ignore us?
The trees rolled their eyes, with a rustle and sway,
As the dandelions joined in the ruckus and play.

Old Ollie the owl, wise but a twit,
Claimed he'd once seen a cow do a split!
The squirrels in stitches, they hollered with glee,
As the shadows danced softly, oh, what a spree!

With blossoms so bright, in a swirl of delight,
The creatures all giggled, till the fall of the night.
From the redbud's embrace, stories flutter and gleam,
Making fun of the world, like a sweet, silly dream.

Songs of the Spiraea

In the garden of giggles, the spiraea bloomed wide,
A frog on a lilly sang with great pride.
He croaked out a tune, a riddle wrapped tight,
About a jump rope and a kite, soaring high in flight.

The bees wore top hats and danced on the breeze,
While the fireflies sparkled like stars with such ease.
They spun in a party, a luminescent glow,
Each twinkle a whisper of fun in the flow.

A hedgehog brought snacks, but all of them rolled,
And the ladybugs laughed, quite brazen and bold.
With crumbs everywhere, the music kept going,
As the playful winds joined, ever sweetly blowing.

From petals to parties, the laughter cascades,
In a circus of petals, where silliness parades.
Every critter's a joker, a dance in the sun,
In the songs of the spiraea, oh, what fun!

Echoes from the Elysium

In a glade full of giggles, the echoes would bounce,
A frog in a bowler gave laughter a flounce.
With tunes from the trees and jokes from the stream,
They crafted a world, a madcap daydream.

The fox with a monocle held court on a rock,
Debating the merits of tick-tock and clock.
With clever retorts, oh, the fun did unfold,
As rabbits spun tales both wild and so bold.

A parrot named Percy, he'd mimic the breeze,
With jokes so absurd, he brought everyone to knees.
The owls in the pines would hoot at their plight,
While the daisies dreamed on in the soft pale moonlight.

So dance through the shadows, let laughter take flight,
In a world that delights in the joys of the night.
With echoes a-buzzing and chirps from below,
The spirit of fun in the heart always grow!

Legends of the Wicked Stem

In a garden where mischief grows,
The thistles laugh at clumsy toes.
They poke and tease, a prickly crew,
Yet charm the bees with skies so blue.

One day a flower lost its crown,
The thistles rolled, they laughed and frowned.
"Your petals droop, what a sad sight!"
But the flower grinned, 'I'll bloom tonight!'

At dusk, they danced, a prickly ball,
With spiky hats that made them tall.
They spun in circles, giggling loud,
As their thorny friends formed quite a crowd.

So listen close, to tales of cheer,
Where laughter grows, and none shed a tear.
The garden blooms with joy, full steam,
In every stem, a funny dream.

Shadows Among the Spiky Veil

Underneath the thorny shade,
A sneaky rabbit's plans were laid.
With thistles as his trusty guide,
He plots a prank with dreamy pride.

A hedgehog watched with widened eyes,
As prickly pals told tangled lies.
"Join us now!" they all would tease,
Their giggles rustled through the leaves.

The rabbit leaped, a daring jump,
Into thorns, with a boisterous thump.
Yet as he fell, they laughed with glee,
"You should have seen your wild spree!"

In corridors of green and gold,
Spiky shadows with stories told.
Among the thorns, where laughter rings,
The garden hums with silly things.

Fables of the Wildflower Heart

In a meadow bright with wild flower hues,
Thistles gathered to share the news.
"A bee just buzzed, so bold and brave!"
"What a clown!" the wildflower gave.

The daisies danced, their petals spread,
As thistles winked and stories fed.
"A tale of charm, a giggle fest,
Our blooms are wild, we know best!"

A bumblebee got lost in flight,
Spinning round in cheerful plight.
"I see you, friend! Fear not, we'll cheer!"
They buzzed and laughed, with naught to fear.

So plant your seeds of fun and cheer,
In every heart, a giggle near.
Among the spines, wild tales adorn,
With petals soft, the laughter's born.

Soliloquy of the Thorned Tale

Beneath the thorns, a story swirls,
Of cheeky weeds and daring curls.
With a flip and flop, they take the stage,
In this wild show, they laugh with rage.

One thistle pranced, a rebel tune,
Dancing round beneath the moon.
"Look at me!" it shouted bold,
"I'm the prickliest of the old!"

The daisies blushed with all their might,
As thistles giggled through the night.
With every twist, the tale grew bright,
In thorny bliss, they took to flight.

So gather round, all weeds and more,
For every thorn, a tale to score.
With humor sharp and laughter free,
In every stem, a mystery.

Ballads of the Bramble Way

In the bramble, a hedgehog sings,
Wearing a crown made of thistle rings.
He danced on his toes, oh what a sight,
With friends all around, the mood was bright.

A butterfly laughed, it tickled his nose,
While a prickle remarked, 'You wear too many clothes!'
They hopped and they skipped, in a tangled row,
In the bramble patch where wild things grow.

The owl hooted softly, 'Watch where you tread,'
As the mushrooms all giggled and some lightly fled.
With a wink and a grin, they planned a parade,
Where thistles and buds would all be displayed.

So gather your friends in the evening's glow,
With laughter and mischief, let the good times flow.
For in the midst of the brambles so spry,
Life rolls on dancing, oh me, oh my!

Chronicles of the Wild Prairie

The prairie dogs pranced in a grand ballet,
With a cowbird conducting, leading the way.
They twirled and they spun, oh what a scene,
In their patch of the grass all bright and green.

A tumbleweed laughed as it rolled on by,
Waving its spindly arms with a sigh.
'Catch me if you can!' it hollered out loud,
As rabbits all giggled and jumped in a crowd.

The crickets played music beneath the moonlight,
While the stars twinkled down, feeling quite bright.
A coyote in costume sang a wild tune,
As the prairie danced under the watchful moon.

With every step taken, stories unfurled,
Each moment together, a new gem to swirled.
In the wild prairie where laughter won't fade,
The chronicles live on in every charade!

The Enchantment of Prickled Dreams

In the garden of dreams where the thistles sway,
A rabbit named Benny lost his way.
He hopped on a thistle, thought it a throne,
Feeling quite royal, yet all was his own.

With a puff of a dandelion, fairies appeared,
Their giggles so sweet that no one would fear.
They twirled 'round the thorns, casting sparkles in flight,
With Benny the bunny, dancing all night.

A wise old tortoise, half-hidden in leaves,
Chortled at Benny, 'What fun it achieves!'
With a flick of his tail, the rabbit would spin,
While thistles all whispered, 'Let the fun begin!'

And in that wild world, of prickles and dreams,
Laughter erupted, bursting at seams.
So come join the storm of the whimsical sprites,
In gardens of laughter, where fun ignites!

Stories Woven in Wild Grasses

In the crickets' choir, a tale begins,
With frolicsome fireflies twisting in spins.
A squirrel stole nuts, but tripped on a vine,
While the grasses all chuckled, 'He'll be just fine!'

A hedgehog played poker with friends made of moss,
Betting on seeds, but losing his sauce.
'You've got no chance!' cried the wise old bee,
As the hedgehog frowned and sipped on his tea.

Then came the wind, blowing wild and free,
Telling tales of mischief and jubilee.
With each twist and turn, the laughter would roll,
In stories of grasses that warmed up the soul.

So gather your pals in the soft twilight,
And weave all your stories till the stars shine bright.
For in the great wild, where grasshoppers play,
Life's finest moments are never in gray!

Parables of the Periwinkle

In a garden where colors meet,
Periwinkle danced on tiny feet.
It tickled the noses of passersby,
With laughter that echoed, oh my, oh my!

A bumblebee buzzed, quite out of tune,
Chasing the petals beneath the moon.
"I swear I can rhyme!" it called with glee,
But tripped on a toad, and fell in a spree!

Worms held a ball under soil so deep,
Where roots told secrets they vowed to keep.
The daisies twirled, their heads held high,
While snails played tag, oh my, oh my!

So heed the lessons from flowers bright,
When you stumble, just laugh, it'll feel all right.
For joy can sprout in the quirkiest ways,
Like periwinkle dancing on sunny days.

Serenade of the Stinging Nettles

In the shade where nettles sing,
The frogs leap high, and the crickets cling.
A nettle named Ned wore a crown of woe,
"Don't touch me!" he yelled, as they watched the show.

The squirrels threw acorns as an encore call,
While the hedgehogs snickered and tried not to fall.
Each prick had a punchline, sharp as a dart,
But laughter was always the best antidote art.

A swing of the breeze sent some leaves in flight,
Tickling the nettles, oh what a sight!
"Do you mind?" they complained, with a rustle and sigh,
"Next time let's dance, but don't make us cry!"

So under the boughs, their humor does bloom,
Remember the nettles, don't be a gloom.
For fun can be found in the prickliest places,
Where even the nettles show off their graces.

The Sonnet of the Sagebrush

Sagebrush swayed in a windy embrace,
With secrets and stories, a curious place.
"I'm not just a plant!" it proudly declared,
"I'm witty and wise, and fully prepared!"

The tumbleweeds laughed, rolled away in a spin,
"Your wisdom is great, but where do we begin?"
With a rustle and chuckle, sage made a stand,
"Life's much more fun when you're part of a band!"

Desert critters gathered, curious and bright,
To hear the sage's tales from morning to night.
"Just sway with the breeze, let your worries run free,
For laughter can echo like waves in the sea!"

And so in the dunes, where the sun paints the sky,
Sagebrush whispered wisdom, and time seemed to fly.
For humor grows wild in the soft, sandy dunes,
Where every sage's jest lights up like the moons.

Poems in the Poppies

In fields of poppies, bright and fair,
The petals danced in sunlit air.
A poet named Pete sat with a sigh,
"Oh, poppies, please, tell me the sky!"

With a giggle, the flowers began to sway,
"We're famed for our dreams, come join the play!"
They whispered secrets, like a breeze on the run,
"Life's full of jest, oh, don't weigh a ton!"

A butterfly flitted, flashing bright blue,
"Don't rush through the blooms, there's magic in dew!"
Each drop held a tale, sticky and sweet,
Like candy that pops with delight in each beat.

So linger in fields, let your laughter spring,
For poetry thrives where the poppies sing.
Life's humor is woven in colors so bright,
Where petals make you chuckle from morning to night.

Whispers of the Willowherb

In fields where whispers fly so free,
A curious bug danced with glee.
He tripped on petals, fell with a thud,
And looked quite silly, splashed in the mud.

The breeze carried giggles, a soft little sound,
As frogs in the pond played leapfrog around.
The flowers all chuckled, their colors ablaze,
While grasshoppers chimed in with their funny phrase.

One thistle remarked, with a wink in its eye,
'Oh, dear bug, must you always be flyin' so high?'
The bug just wiggled, adjusted his wings,
Said, 'I dance for the fun that this mischief brings!'

With every new tumble, the laughter would swell,
In the land of the thistle, all was quite well.
For even in stumbles, delight we could find,
In the jests of the meadow, we leave woes behind.

The Saga of the Scabious

In a patch of scabious, fluff and delight,
A snail named Eric took an unusual flight.
He climbed on a petal, so lofty and grand,
Proclaiming, 'Behold! I'm the king of this land!'

The daisies all giggled, their heads bent down low,
While bees buzzed loudly, putting on quite a show.
Eric soon slipped, with a twist and a spin,
And landed quite softly, a grin on his chin.

'Fear not!' shouted Eric, 'For I still reign supreme!'
The flowers erupted, a collective loud beam.
The snails just keep sliding, they slip with such grace,
In the saga of scabious, there's humor in space.

So raise up your cups for this humorous chap,
In this garden of giggles, let's all take a nap.
For life's a wild ride in the blooms that entice,
With laughter and sunshine, it's all very nice.

Fables of the Foxglove

In a forest of foxgloves, bright bells would ring,
A squirrel named Chuck thought he could sing.
He climbed to the top, and with all of his might,
He croaked out a tune that gave owls a fright.

The petals all quaked in a fluttery fuss,
As critters gathered round, in a giggly rush.
Chuck took a deep breath, gave a final loud shout,
And promptly fell backward—oh, what a clout!

The rabbits erupted, their laughter a song,
'Oh Chuck, your voice isn't really that strong!'
But Chuck just grinned, with eyes like a spark,
'At least I'm a star in this woodland park!'

So let every creature, from large to quite small,
Join in on the fun; it's a party for all.
For in foxglove fields, where joy does abound,
There's a harmony found in the laughter profound.

The Poetics of the Pansy

In the garden of pansies, a poet would sneeze,
While scribbling sonnets beneath the great trees.
The flower peered over, with petals so sly,
'Bless you, dear poet! But why do you cry?'

The poet replied with a chuckle and grin,
'I write of your beauty, and all that you've been!
But those who read poems, they shake their bright heads,
Saying blooms can't talk, they just fill up with spreads!'

The pansy just giggled, her colors so bright,
'Fear not, fickle reader, I'm here to excite!
With stories of laughter and petals that gleam,
Let's turn all these frowns to a burst of a dream.'

So the poet kept writing, each word a delight,
In the poetics of pansies, all worries took flight.
With every new stanza, the humor would flow,
In a garden of whimsy, where joy's sure to grow.

Voices of the Verbena

In gardens where the verbena sway,
The flowers giggle, come what may.
With whispers shared among the bees,
They mock the breeze and tease the trees.

A ladybug in polka dots,
Claims flower crowns and sways a lot.
The daisies chuckle, oh so wide,
While petals dance with glee and pride.

The thyme complains of being late,
As ants parade and celebrate.
Together they sing a flowery tune,
Beneath the chuckling sun and moon.

When rain drops fall, they hold a feast,
For every bug, they're quite the beast.
So if you pause and lean real near,
You'll hear their giggles, loud and clear.

Truths Carved in the Thistles

Among the thistles, sharp and loud,
The creatures jest, so very proud.
A hedgehog tells a tale absurd,
Of fish that fly and sheep that herd.

A rabbit winks and claims it true,
That carrots grow on trees, not through.
With prickly jokes and puns galore,
Their chuckles echo, evermore.

Beneath the spines, a party brews,
With thistle punch and prickly brews.
The beetles dance in swirly spins,
While laughter bubbles, where fun begins.

So heed the thistle's tales tonight,
For truths unwind in sheer delight.
In every quip, there's wisdom spry,
Just look and laugh, don't ask me why.

The Poetry of the Pineapple Weed

In fields where pineapple weed does grow,
The critters gather for the show.
With rhymes that bounce and twirl about,
They sing of jellybeans, no doubt.

A frog in glasses reads aloud,
To an audience of bugs, so proud.
They clap their wings and stomp their feet,
For silly lines can't be beat!

The grasshoppers join in the fun,
Leaping high under the sun.
With every hop, they share a quirk,
As laughter dances, it's quite the perk.

So if you're feeling kind of blue,
Just find a weed that's bright and new.
Join in the laughter, sing along,
For poetry lives where hearts are strong.

Legends of the Laborador Tea

In corners dense with laborador tea,
The gossip flows, oh so carefree.
A squirrel spins tales of nutty sights,
Of acorns dressed in fancy lights.

The butterflies nod, with knowing winks,
Claiming all the wisdom from their drinks.
While ladybugs debate the best,
On leaf-shaped chairs, they take their rest.

A wise old owl joins in the chat,
Sipping slowly, how about that!
With tales of mischief and of grace,
They share a laugh, a warm embrace.

So brew a cup and take a seat,
In forest halls, life's quite the treat.
For legends whispered, sweet as pie,
Will tickle your heart and make you cry!

Folklore of the Ferns

In a forest of ferns, quite lush,
Danced a squirrel with a sudden rush.
He twirled 'round a rock,
And slipped on a sock,
Leaving critters in laughter and hush.

A bear tried to join in the cheer,
Tripped over roots, oh dear! Oh dear!
With a flop and a roll,
He caused quite a toll,
As the woodland folks laughed and drew near.

The wise old owl gave a hoot,
At the sight of a clumsy brute.
He chuckled aloud,
To the gathering crowd,
As they cheered for the bear's funny loot.

So if you find ferns on your way,
Listen close for the jests they say.
Nature's grand comics,
With antics so iconic,
Will brighten your dull, dreary day.

Stories Beneath the Sunflower

Beneath the sun's glorious glow,
Sunflowers sway to and fro.
They gossip and tease,
In the warm summer breeze,
Spinning tales only they know.

A bee buzzed too loudly one day,
As he danced on a petal in play.
He slipped on some dew,
With a "Whee! Look at you!"
And landed right smack in the hay.

A worm, with great dreams in his mind,
Thought he'd leave all his worries behind.
He wriggled and squirmed,
Till the daisies confirmed,
That sunflowers' laughter's one of a kind.

So if you stroll past a patch,
Listen closely, you may catch:
A story or two,
From the flowers so true,
In their giggles, you'll find quite a match.

Ballads of the Brambles

In a thicket of brambles and thorns,
A rabbit was playing with horns.
He squeaked out a tune,
On a flashy monsoon,
While the hedgehogs applauded, forlorn.

A crafty old fox joined the show,
In a top hat, he stole the whole flow.
He jived with delight,
Till he slipped in the night,
And landed in brambles below!

The birds circled round for a laugh,
While the rabbit just flaunted his craft.
With a wink and a grin,
They sang once again,
As the brambles bore witness, by half.

So heed this peculiar refrain,
Where the brambles hold laughter like rain.
In the wild garden's sway,
Every whimsy at play,
Turns mischief to joy, not in vain.

The Mystery of the Morning Glory

A morning glory wore a grand hat,
Claiming to be the poshest of that.
But a butterfly teased,
"You're quite over-dressed!",
'Cause you bloom with a sleepy-eyed spat.

With each dawn, she pranced in a show,
Chasing shadows, where nobody'd go.
But a gopher appeared,
With laughter he smeared,
"Are you waking, or simply too slow?"

The bees buzzed, all charm and delight,
As they chuckled at morning's bright sight.
"Oh, what a fine plan,
To be late, if you can!"
And they laughed as they danced with pure light.

So next time you wake with a yawn,
Remember the blooms heralding dawn.
Life's funny, you see,
Full of whimsy and glee,
In a garden where giggles are drawn.

www.ingramcontent.com/pod-product-compliance
Lightning Source LLC
Chambersburg PA
CBHW071824160426
43209CB00003B/206